MAP OF STONEHENGE AND SURROUNDING AREA

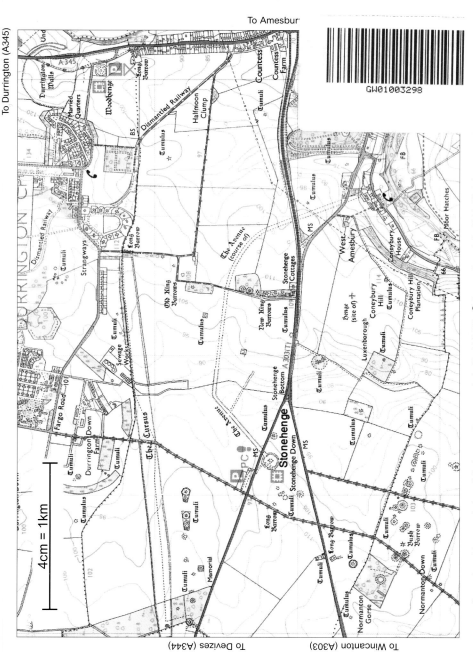

To Amesbury

To Durrington (A345)

4cm = 1km

To Devizes (A344)

To Wincanton (A303)

To Normanton Down

1

INTRODUCTION

Stonehenge is unique. What we see standing on the near bare Salisbury Plain today is a ruin that is dwarfed not only by the landscape but also by its reputation. Although there are other prehistoric stone circles in Britain none of them display the same levels of achievement as Stonehenge. Engineering skills that were thought to be beyond Stone Age man were used to transport, erect and secure the stones.

It took well over 1,000 years to develop through several stages of wooden and stone settings. Only basic tools were used in its construction, and the planning, patience and dedication spent on it must have required a huge

> As long as ten thousand years ago the area around Stonehenge was a sacred place

amount of time. Stone Age people, with an average lifespan of only 35 years, carried out the work knowing that they would never see the project completed in their lifetime.

A relationship between the living and the dead seems to be a reoccurring theme in monuments of this age. It has been estimated that the cremated remains of approximately 240 people have been buried within the site.

Over many years a large number of experts have studied the monument and their work

forms the basis of what is known. Because it is so old and its construction took place over such a long time it is often very difficult to interpret what all the findings mean.

However one thing seems certain, and that is the alignment with the midsummer sunrise. This well-known fact has encouraged people to speculate about what it was used for and what other secrets it still may hold. For as long as anyone can remember people have attempted to explain the mystery of Stonehenge.

Many claims have been made for it, but it is best thought of as a temple, a place for communal gatherings at important times of the year. It lies in an area that was not used for domestic purposes, and as long ago as five thousand years before there was any building at Stonehenge there is evidence that the area was being used as a sacred place.

The name Stonehenge has been in use since about 1130AD and is thought to have originated from 'hanging stones'. It could have been a reference to the suspended lintels, or because the structure resembled a series of gallows. The term henge has a much broader meaning now and has become the collective name for any sacred circular enclosure consisting of a bank and ditch.

Most prehistoric sites are roughly circular in shape. Ancient people may have chosen to build circles as a symbol of a never-ending cycle of birth and rebirth, or perhaps they mirrored the two circles in the sky - the sun and the moon. They were also a fairly simple shape to mark out using only a length of rope and fixed peg.

Stonehenge attracts nearly a million visitors each year and most come with some idea of what it is all about. Although the most studied of all prehistoric monuments there are still many questions that remain unanswered. Excavations at the many other prehistoric sites in the area have provided a greater insight to the people who lived all those years ago. It is the people and their customs that are the key to understanding Stonehenge.

The cremated remains of about 240 ancient people are buried at Stonehenge

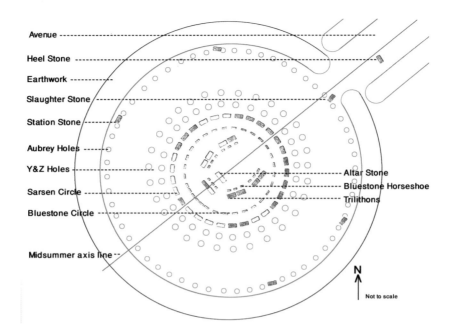

Labels (top to bottom, left side): Avenue, Heel Stone, Earthwork, Slaughter Stone, Station Stone, Aubrey Holes, Y&Z Holes, Sarsen Circle, Bluestone Circle, Midsummer axis line

Labels (right side): Altar Stone, Bluestone Horseshoe, Trilithons

N

Not to scale

THE MAIN FEATURES

Stonehenge has many features made from both earth and stone. The stones are of two different types, neither of which are from the area. The larger ones are sarsens and came from about 20 miles (30km) away, near another stone circle at Avebury. The other smaller stones are bluestones and were transported from the Preseli Mountains in Wales.

Starting from the outside of the monument and working in you will find:

The Avenue

Leading to the monument from the north-east and crossed by the road are two parallel ditches and low banks, which are thought to mark a processional way to Stonehenge. Although this part of the Avenue is straight further away it turns to the right and eventually meets the River Avon. This path may have been used for people to approach Stonehenge at special times or may even have been the route along which the stones themselves were moved to the site.

The Heel Stone

Standing lonely by the road near the head of the Avenue, this unshaped piece of sarsen was thought to mark the position of the sunrise on the longest day of the year. In fact it once had a partner, and the sun was framed between the two stones as it made its way over the horizon.

Only 50 of the original 84 sarsens are left at Stonehenge

4

The Slaughter Stone

At the main entrance through the earthwork is a fallen sarsen known as the Slaughter Stone. Earlier visitors, who believed the builders of Stonehenge were savages, conjured images of sacrifices on this stone and the stained indentations reinforced the idea. In fact it once stood upright along with others and the stains are the result of rainwater reacting with naturally occurring iron within the stone.

The Earthwork

This is often overlooked at first with the stones taking all the attention. About 30 metres (100ft) outside the stones are the remains of the bank and ditch. The earthwork is unusual because it is the only known enclosure of this type to have its bank on the inside of the ditch. It has two entrances - the main one that leads out to the Avenue in the direction of the midsummer sunrise and a secondary one to the south. Over time the bank has eroded and the ditch has filled up.

The Station Stones

There were once four Station Stones positioned just inside the bank. Two are still visible, one

The Heel Stone

standing, the other fallen. Some time after they were erected two of them were surrounded by shallow circular ditches and banks. Although they are not thought to have contained burials, they are known as the North and South Barrows.

The Aubrey Holes

These holes, first noticed by John Aubrey (1626-97), have been covered with white cement and lie in a circle inside the bank in line with the Station Stones. There are 56 of them and are thought to have held wooden posts in the first phase of the site long before the stones were ever erected. Around half of them have been investigated and some have revealed cremated human remains thought to have been placed there after the holes were no longer used for their original purpose.

'Y' and 'Z' Holes

Invisible to us now, two more rings of holes were discovered between the Aubrey Holes and the stones. They never seem to have been put to use, but it has been suggested that they were intended for bluestones.

Sarsen Circle

When complete this was a magnificent continuous ring of 30 stone lintels supported by 30 uprights. Seventeen of these still stand, and each one weighs approximately 25 tonnes. Craftsmanship and design are seen in the way the lintels are shaped. Each one is slightly curved to soften otherwise angular

Sarsen is a type of sandstone toughened with silica

Sarsen circle with smaller bluestones inside

Trilithon

edges and held in place with carved joints. Although the stones are large, they seem even larger because of clever use of perspective.

The Bluestone Circle

Inside the sarsen circle are the remains of a ring of about 60 smaller upright bluestones. Some of these stones show signs of having been used before as lintels either at Stonehenge or perhaps before they were moved from Wales.

The Trilithons

These are the freestanding doorway-like features with two uprights and one lintel across the top. The name means three stones, and there were once five of these structures with the largest in the middle and the others each stepping down in size. The tallest stone at Stonehenge is 22 feet high and is the one remaining upright of what was the largest trilithon. Its tenon, which was used to hold the lintel in place, can be clearly seen protruding from the top. In front lies the lintel with corresponding mortice holes.

The Bluestone Horseshoe

The remaining stones of a smaller horseshoe of about 19 upright bluestones lies within the sarsen trilithons.

The Altar Stone

This stone once stood as a pillar, and would have been the focal point of the entire monument. As the sun rose on midsummer's day its light would strike this stone. It now lies fallen and half buried in the ground astride the midsummer axis line, and was thought by earlier visitors to have been used as an altar.

View from Slaughter Stone

BUILDING STONEHENGE

Stonehenge evolved over a period of more than 1,000 years, and was constructed using the most basic of tools such as antler picks, ox shoulder blade shovels and plant fibre ropes. It was constantly being changed and improved, not just extended but on several occasions completely dismantled and repositioned. Techniques that were learned over generations were passed on and used to create grander and more complex structures.

Because the site was developed over such a long time its erection is usually divided into three phases:

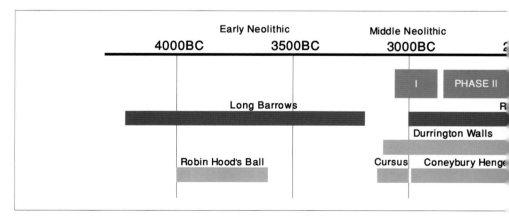

Phase 1
Around 5,000 years ago

Before any stones were erected the bank and ditch were dug in a roughly circular shape. The ditch was not continuous but made up of several trenches with steep sides and flat bottoms. The chalk rubble was thrown up on the inside of the ditch to create a bank that measured about 1.8 metres (6ft) high.

Even at this early stage the evidence of the sun's importance is obvious. Two entrances were left in the earthwork and the main one faced north-east towards the midsummer sunrise.

On the inside of the white chalk bank a circle of 56 wooden posts was raised.

Phase 2
Between 4,900 and 4,500 years ago

During this phase the wooden posts, which by now were rotten, were removed and the empty post-holes began to be used for

cremated remains. Other posts were erected within the circle, but their purpose is unknown. They may have been used as markers for the sun and moon, or could possibly have been the uprights of timber buildings.

Phase 3
Between 4,500 and 3,600 years ago

This is the phase of stone structures and lasted for nearly 1,000 years.

The last of the timber posts were removed and two bluestone crescents were set up, one inside the other.

Probably several centuries later four sarsen stones were placed around the inside of the bank, and what is known as the Heel Stone and its missing partner were erected outside the earthwork on the line of the midsummer axis.

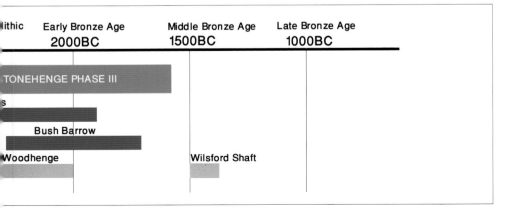

lithic	Early Bronze Age 2000BC	Middle Bronze Age 1500BC	Late Bronze Age 1000BC
TONEHENGE PHASE III			
s			
Bush Barrow			
Woodhenge		Wilsford Shaft	

Shaped bluestone

At around the same time the Altar Stone was raised in the centre of the circle and was positioned to face the gap between the two Heel Stones.

Sometime later again the bluestones were removed and reused in what was to become their final position. The huge sarsens were brought in and used to build the linked sarsen circle and the horseshoe of even larger trilithons. The bluestones were used for a corresponding circle and horseshoe inside their sarsen counterparts.

The Avenue was also created at this time and, because it leads down to the River Avon, it is thought that it may have been used for the transportation of the stones to the site. This process may even have been part of a ritual.

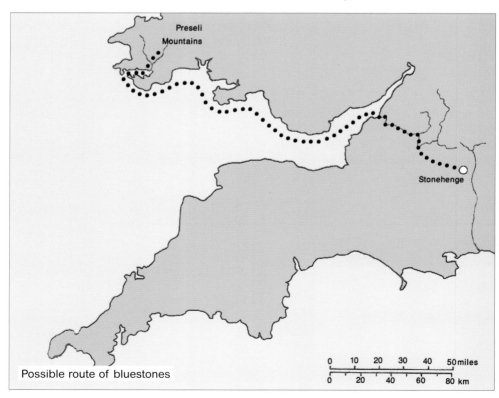
Preseli Mountains

Stonehenge

| 0 | 10 | 20 | 30 | 40 | 50 miles |
| 0 | 20 | 40 | 60 | 80 km |

Possible route of bluestones

10

Sarsens in their natural setting

Transporting the Stones

The most likely way the bluestones were transported from the Preseli Mountains in south-west Wales to Salisbury Plain was by boat from Milford Haven. The boat would probably have hugged the coastline until crossing the Bristol Channel. Here they may have continued by boat all the way around the Cornish coast, or transferred the stone to a raft and journeyed up the Bristol Avon then dragged the stone the remaining distance overland using sledges or wooden rollers.

Although the sarsens originated much closer, they were much bigger and there was still a lot of ground to cover. Modern experiments have shown that perhaps only four people were needed to move a stone by water and probably more than 100 to drag one overland. So it is likely the River Avon was used and, if this were the case, then the sarsens may have been unloaded at the end of the Avenue.

If not, they were dragged about 20miles (30km) over the hills and valleys between the two sites.

Shaping the Stones

Almost all of the stones at Stonehenge have been shaped. Their sides were smoothed using round balls of sarsen called mauls and, as it is an extremely hard stone, only tiny fragments would have been scraped off at a time.

The upright sarsens were tapered slightly towards the top to make them appear taller and more impressive. As well as this the top surface was left with two protruding knobs called

> All the sarsens are shaped except the Heel Stone and the Station Stones

Mortice Hole

tenons, which were used to secure the lintels.

Each 9 tonne lintel was also cleverly shaped. Not only were corresponding mortice holes carved into their underside they also had a ridge carved on one end and a groove on the other so each one would fit snugly and securely with the next. These joints are more usual in woodworking and are not seen in any other prehistoric stone circle.

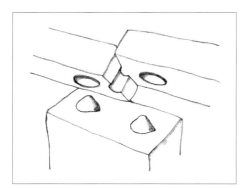

The subtle curve of the lintels completes the effect of a smooth and uninterrupted circle, which in a less sophisticated design would have been a series of straight lines. All these factors required a great deal of forethought and planning.

Erecting the Stones

The first step for raising a stone was to dig the hole it would sit in. The depth of the hole would be adjusted for each stone to make sure the tops would be level.

The base would be manoeuvred over the hole and hauled upright by about 200 men using ropes and poles. The base would then be packed with stone fragments, old mauls and chalk rubble to make it secure.

Stonehenge was built over forty generations

12

Two methods have been suggested for getting the lintels into their positions. The first involved pulling the stone up a huge temporary ramp made from soil and chalk. With this method the ramp would have to be dug out and rebuilt in a slightly different place for each lintel.

The other involved raising the stone inch by inch with levers. First the stone was positioned next to the uprights, and then alternate ends of the stone would be levered up and supported with a wooden plank. The next layer of planks would be laid crossways to give the structure stability. Then this process would be repeated until the wooden crib supporting the stone was level with the top of the

Sarsen smoothed with mauls

One lintel weighs the same as a double-decker bus

uprights. The lintel would be moved sideways and lowered on to the protruding tenons.

Tallest stone with protruding tenon

THE DRUIDS

Stonehenge and Druids were first linked together in the 1600s. The thinking was simple: Stonehenge was a temple and the Druids were an ancient priesthood.

In the first century AD the Romans wrote about the Druids. They recorded them to be widely established throughout Britain and that they were a Celtic priesthood of a nature-based religion. They were not known for building temples but conducted their rituals in forest clearings. To them the oak tree was sacred and mistletoe, especially that grown on an oak, was particularly important.

Two thousand years before this Stonehenge was being built. Druid priests may well have been

> Druidism is a Celtic nature based religion

present, after all Christianity and other religions have been practiced for an equal or longer length of time, but there is no evidence that supports the view that Druids were the builders of Stonehenge. If they were you have to wonder what could have happened to make them abandon a temple, which was the result of the efforts of generations, and revert to worshipping in forests again.

The antiquarian William Stukeley, who closely studied Stonehenge in the early 1700s, believed that Stonehenge was a Druidic temple and later became obsessed with the idea of Druidism. He began to consider himself one and styled himself as the Grand Arch-Druid.

New interest in the ancient religion began a revival and in 1781 a secret society, 'The Ancient Order of the Druids' was formed

Stonehenge by William Stukeley

Ancient Order of the Druids 1905

by gentlemen in much the same vein as the Freemasons. At their meetings they dressed in the white hooded robes described by the Romans, wore long false beards and carried sickles for cutting mistletoe. This group visited Stonehenge for the first time in 1905.

There was at least one other

group calling themselves Druids who had been carrying out their rituals at Stonehenge before this. When an admission fee began to be charged these Druids refused to pay for access to what they believed was their temple and led the protests against it. There were many clashes between them and the landowners but eventually, after many years, access was permitted again.

They had, after all, been using Stonehenge for ceremonies for sometime and even if it was an adopted place of worship it was, and still is, their chosen place to practise their religion.

Today modern Druids are as much a part of the solstice spectacle as the sunrise. They still follow the nature-based religion and dress in hooded cloaks for ceremonies though the beards, if worn, tend to be real. They strongly believe they have an ancient connection with Stonehenge and are allowed access at summer solstice to perform their rituals.

ASTRONOMY

For centuries it has been recognised that Stonehenge has a connection with the sun. During a one-year cycle the sun rises and sets in a slightly different position each day so only on the 21st June does it rise in the north-east over (or next to) the Heel Stone. As the longest day of the year it marks the turning of the seasons when daylight hours once again begin to shorten. The sun appears to rise here for a few days before starting its return journey through the sky.

Thousands of years ago the midwinter sunset, now usually seen on the 21st December, may have been even more important than the midsummer sunrise. Seen in reverse, the setting sun was framed by the central trilithon

Midwinter sunset

along the same sight line. The event would mark a time when the daylight would begin to increase, and that would have been a welcome sign in the dark winter months. It was the beginning of a new year and a time to celebrate.

The midway points between these two solstices are called the spring and autumn equinox. They happen on or around the 21st March and 21st September. On

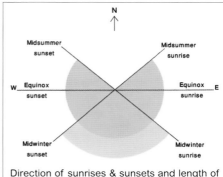

Direction of sunrises & sunsets and length of daylight hours during summer and winter

these two days the sun rises and sets exactly east and west making the day and night equal in length.

These important times in the year are still recognised and are celebrated in the Christian calendar as Easter and harvest festival.

The people who built Stonehenge would have been much more aware of what was happening in the sky than people today would generally be.

The sun was obviously important. It rose every day without fail giving varying degrees of light and warmth. With so much of their lives depending on these things it is easy to see how the sun was revered and rituals performed to try to please it.

If the sun was worshipped then maybe the moon was too. Both had the power to light up the world, and moved silently across the sky.

Stonehenge is aligned with the longest and shortest days of the year

The cycles of the moon are far more complicated than the sun. Not only does it go through a 29½ day lunar month, from new moon to full through to new moon again, but also it rises and sets at different points on the horizon. To fully complete its journey across the sky takes 18.6 years.

If lines are drawn to join the Station Stones they form a rectangle, which neatly contains the stone circle. The longest sides of the rectangle seem to be aligned with the moon's most southerly moonrise and its most northerly moonset, and the short sides are parallel with the midsummer axis through Stonehenge.

So was Stonehenge a sort of calendar marking the important times in the year, or was it, as others have claimed, an even more sophisticated machine?

The moon takes 29½ days to complete a lunar month, and over 18 years to travel though a full lunar cycle

In the 1960s book, 'Stonehenge Decoded' Gerald S. Hawkins claimed that the 56 Aubrey Holes were used for predicting eclipses. The number 56 represented three moon cycles, two cycles of 19 years each and one of 18 years to bring the count back into line. This is not unlike our extra day during a leap year. This combination, he claimed, was the most accurate way of measuring the cycles in whole numbers.

If stone markers had been placed in the Aubrey Holes and moved anticlockwise one hole a year they could fairly accurately have predicted when an eclipse would happen.

Heel Stone from the centre of Stonehenge

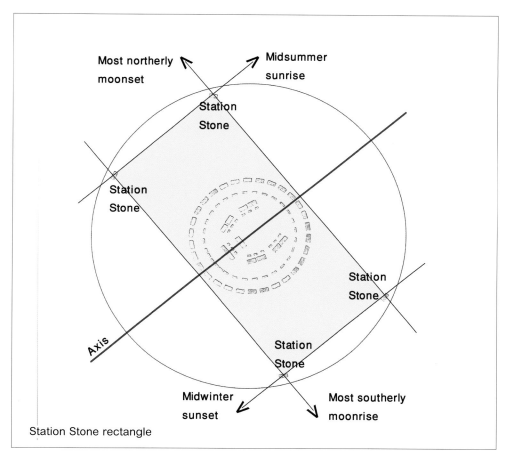

Most northerly moonset

Midsummer sunrise

Station Stone

Station Stone

Station Stone

Axis

Station Stone

Midwinter sunset

Most southerly moonrise

Station Stone rectangle

Eclipses may have been frightening or religious experiences. They may have been seen as a message from the gods. If a way of predicting these unusual occurrences in the sky were found it would have meant a great deal of power and influence.

Mr Hawkins theories caused quite a stir around the world. It was what people wanted to hear - Stonehenge explained at last!

Many archaeologists have disputed these claims because the holes were filled with cremated remains soon after the posts were removed, which would have made it difficult for them to have held stone markers.

Nevertheless, the idea of Stonehenge as an astronomical observatory has remained in the public's imagination as most people want to believe that there is more to Stonehenge than first meets the eye.

The Aubrey Holes may have been used to predict lunar eclipses

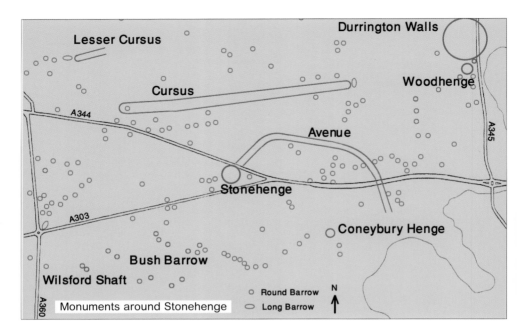

Monuments around Stonehenge

AROUND STONEHENGE

The area around Stonehenge must have been of special importance because a large number of prehistoric sites are nearby. Stonehenge is a centrepiece with the others often being overlooked in favour of their more famous neighbour.

They are not as obvious because their features were made of wood and earth and these, unlike stone, have not lasted throughout the millennia. But this does not make them any less worthy of investigation. Many of them were in use at the same time as Stonehenge was being built, and also have an alignment with the midsummer sunrise. To get to know more about Stonehenge it is sensible to try and understand what was happening in the surrounding landscape.

Mesolithic Post-Holes

Only metres from Stonehenge are four huge post-holes. They are now covered and marked as painted white discs on the car park tarmac. The enormous holes held pine posts about 10,000 years ago, around 5,000 years before the first phase of Stonehenge. They were 2 metres (6½ft) wide and about 15 metres (50ft) tall. This shows that the area was used as a sacred place for an extremely long time.

Robin Hood's Ball

With the exception of the Mesolithic post-holes, this is the earliest of the sites in the area. It is a causewayed enclosure that was used long before the building of Stonehenge as a centre for the community.

It lies 3 miles (5km) north-west of Stonehenge in an army training area that is out of bounds to the general public. The limited excavations carried out have found the ditch filled with broken pottery, animal bones and human remains including skulls. These items are an indication that feasting and funerary rites were held here.

The Stonehenge Cursus

About ½ mile (¾ km) north of Stonehenge is the Cursus. The name is misleading because it implies that it is Roman. In fact, it is probably older than Stonehenge. It is a linear earthwork of two rough-ly parallel banks and ditches which are about 100 metres (330 ft) apart and nearly two miles long (3km). William Stukeley, who named it in the eighteenth century, imagined it was used as a racecourse, but its

purpose can only be guessed.

There is a similar but much smaller version, known as the Lesser Cursus, a little further west. Unfortunately there is nothing left to see of it on the ground and its imprint can only be picked up from crop marks in aerial photographs.

Durrington Walls

This enclosure is the largest henge earthwork in Britain.

It lies north-east of Stonehenge near to Woodhenge and was being used during the time of Stonehenge's construction.

Excavations were carried out in the 1960s on the strip of land that was to be used for a new road. They uncovered the post-holes of two multi-ringed

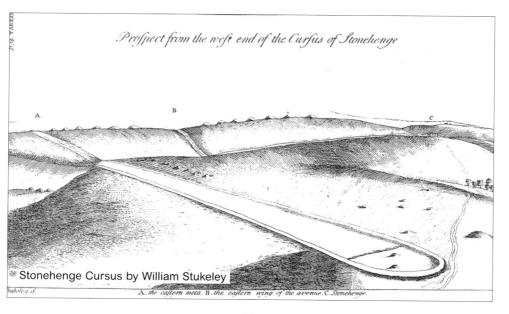

Prospect from the west end of the Cursus of Stonehenge

Stonehenge Cursus by William Stukeley

A. the eastern meta. B. the eastern wing of the avenue. C. Stonehenge.

timber circles, similar to those at Woodhenge. Since then a geophysical survey has confirmed that there are other enclosures within the henge.

Hearths were discovered in the ditch and a large amount of domesticated pig bones led experts to believe that this site was used for feasting. It is possible that this was a place where the workers were fed and the everyday rituals performed.

Recently, further evidence of a close link with Stonehenge was found when a road made of compacted chalk was discovered leading from the south-east entrance directly to the River Avon. Only a short distance along the river lies the end of the Avenue. Could this have been a ceremonial route to Stonehenge?

Woodhenge

Just outside Durrington Walls lies another ceremonial site that was not discovered until 1925 when the pilot of an aircraft noticed rings of dark circles in the grass whilst flying overhead.

The site was investigated further and six oval rings of post-holes were uncovered inside a bank and ditch with an opening facing the midsummer sunrise.

The holes had held oak posts, giving the site its name, yet it is unknown if they had supported lintels or if they were freestanding. It has been suggested that the timbers may have supported a roof although current archaeological thinking is against this.

The post-holes are now marked by short concrete bollards of various diameters that correspond to the actual widths of the posts.

In the centre of these rings is the grave of a three or four year old child. It is claimed by the discoverers of the skeleton that the skull had been split in two, giving rise to speculation that this

Durrington Walls

Woodhenge

was a human sacrifice. Unfortunately no further tests on the bones are possible as they were lost during the Second World War.

Coneybury Henge

The crop marks that identified Coneybury Henge were initially thought to have been a levelled round barrow. When investigated, it was revealed to be an oval shaped henge monument with an entrance aligned with the midsummer sunrise. It is situated less than a mile (just over 1km) to the south-east of Stonehenge on Coneybury Hill. Again, due to ploughing, there is not much to see on the ground. It was built in a woodland clearing, and inside its bank and ditch were the familiar ring of posts set at regular intervals. It was in use at the same time as Stonehenge although for some reason it was abandoned and became overgrown after only a fairly brief period of use.

Wilsford Shaft

South-west of Stonehenge a deep shaft was discovered during the excavation of what appeared to be a pond barrow. The shaft was over 30 metres (100ft) deep and 2 metres (6½ ft) wide.

This shaft appeared at first to have been used as a well as ropes and buckets were found at its waterlogged bottom, but later it seemed to have served another purpose. For some reason the hole was deliberately filled in with layers of ritual deposits including bone needles and jewellery.

Flints for arrows and tools were mined in the area

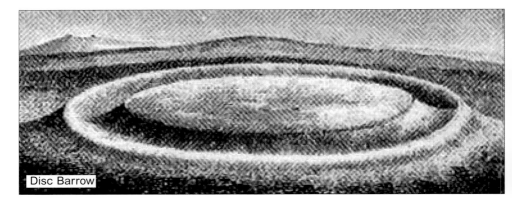
Disc Barrow

BARROWS

Barrows are burial mounds, and there are a significant number of them in the area around Stonehenge where they appear more densely than in any other part of the country.

Long Barrows

The earliest forms were the long barrows. These were built in the Early Neolithic period between 6,000 and 5,000 years ago before even the first phase of Stonehenge.

Long Barrow

They were long chambered tombs usually with wooden supports and some had stone chambers within. The bones of the dead were only placed in these tombs after the flesh had either rotted or been stripped away. Complete skeletons were rarely found intact.

The best example in the Stonehenge area is at the Winterbourne Stoke roundabout, just off the A303. There is a good selection of all the different types of barrow in this group.

Round Barrows

Although a large number can still be seen throughout Wessex many have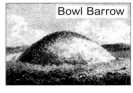
Bowl Barrow
been ploughed out over the centuries. They are often found in linear groups on top of ridges and come in an assortment of shapes. These are named accordingly as Bowl, Bell, Pond and Disc Barrows.

These types were in use during the second and third phases of Stonehenge.

Saucer Barrow

Unfortunately most of them had been robbed by the time of the early antiquarians so not much is known about any treasure that was found in them.

The robbers were not inclined to take bones, and whole skeletons were found in the earlier types of round barrow. They were not laid out straight, as is customary now, but were often found in a crouched or foetal position, possibly symbolising their return to mother earth.

Later examples, including the now rare pond-barrows, contained cremated remains in either a small pit or container.

Bush Barrow

In September 1808 Richard Colt Hoare and William Cunnington were excavating a barrow known as Bush Barrow when they made an extraordinary discovery. They found a complete skeleton of a tall stout man laid out with his feet pointing towards Stonehenge.

Bell Barrow

Arranged around him were the finest treasures, and they realised they had found a barrow that had not already been plundered. There were a bronze axe and three bronze daggers, similar to those carved on the sarsens at Stonehenge, along with the remains of a shield with bronze rivets, and other unused weapons. One of the daggers was extremely finely crafted with thousands of tiny gold rivets set in a zigzag pattern on the handle. A large gold diamond-shaped plate, possibly a breastplate, with geometric designs was also found with a smaller gold plate and a gold buckle.

It can be assumed that the man buried in this barrow was one of great importance. He may have been a great chief who ruled the area and who was closely linked with Stonehenge.

Bell Barrow

CARVINGS ON THE STONES

There are many carvings on the sarsen stones at Stonehenge. Some of them are graffiti from the last century, but there are others thought to have been made around 3,800 years ago during the Early Bronze Age.

The engravings of 40 axe-heads and one dagger were first noticed in 1953 on the inner side of one of the great trilithon stones and on two other sarsens in the outer circle.

They are similar to the axe-heads and daggers found in Bush Barrow situated only ⅔ mile (1km) away from Stonehenge and are typical of Bronze Age carvings found at other burial sites.

It seems that axes may have had a symbolic meaning as well as practical purposes because some have been found made of highly prized materials that were not suitable to work with.

The axe head carvings all point to the sky, which may be significant, and range from 8cm (3ins) to 36cm (14ins) in length. They were photographed when discovered, but were never fully studied until recently.

In 2003 new laser technology was used to map the surface of these three stones. The pictures showed there are many other axe-head carvings on them, but sadly they are so badly eroded they are invisible to the naked eye.

It seems that the possibility of more hidden carvings on other stones is quite likely and further research in this area may even throw fresh light onto the purpose of Stonehenge.

Lasers have shown there are many more carvings than previously thought

Dagger and axe-head carving

Tourists

VISITORS

The coach tours that are a daily feature at Stonehenge today were just as popular in Victorian times. A carriage could be hired from Salisbury for the day that would take you to Old Sarum in the morning and on to Stonehenge in the afternoon.

The coachmen running the tours wanted their paying customers to be impressed, but unfortunately they often were not. Because Stonehenge could be glimpsed from afar, by the time the coach had finally covered the full distance all sense of wonder had gone.

The coachmen overcame this problem by drawing down the window shutters and raised them theatrically on arrival so the full effect could be appreciated.

For those who arrived on horseback, the 'Shepherd of Salisbury Plain' would offer to hold horses for a few shillings and tell stories about the stones. There was a legend that no one could count the stones and come up with the same number twice. This game became a popular pastime at the stones.

A well-prepared tourist would bring their own picnic to be eaten within the circle, using the stones as seats and tables, and discarding their chicken bones and beer bottles on the ground. For the not so organised refreshments could be bought at Amesbury where one could also hire a hammer to chip off a piece of Stonehenge to take home.

Hammers were used to remove souvenir pieces of stone during Victorian times

Stonehenge by Constable

A less damaging souvenir was a photograph, and Stonehenge was one of the first places to offer a snap of the visitor posing in front of the stones. This is something that tourists can still be seen doing today. Even before photography sketches would usually contain someone in the foreground in the 'I was here' pose.

Although the Victorians popularised tourism, there are records of day-trippers as early as the reign of Queen Elizabeth I (1533-1603).

Many famous people have been to the stones since then. Royalty included James I, Charles II and Queen Victoria herself.

Samuel Pepys (1633-1703) mentioned his visit in his famous diary, and the naturalist Charles Darwin (1809-82) used Stonehenge to conduct experiments with worms.

One of the problems with visitors is that they tend to leave their rubbish behind. Litter is not a modern invention, it has been discarded at Stonehenge since the Iron Age. From this we can see that the place was receiving visitors even then. Although the Romans did not settle nearby items from this period were found showing that they too were curious about the stones. And so it has continued throughout the ages to the modern day when nearly a million people a year pay to visit Stonehenge.

The current facilities at the visitor centre are no longer adequate and do nothing to enhance the visitor's experience. Plans to bury the main road and move the parking and visitors centre further away are being discussed. If a solution to the problems can be found it will give people a chance to fully appreciate Stonehenge in a more natural setting.

Stonehenge was receiving foreign visitors as early as Roman times

SUMMER SOLSTICE CELEBRATIONS

People began gathering again at Stonehenge to watch the sunrise on the longest day of the year when it was noted in the early 1700's.

In 1680 royal approval was given for an annual fair to be held at Stonehenge. Initially it took place in late September, but was moved to the solstice after crowds began to gather at the site to watch the sunrise.

By the late 1800s it was a popular outing and about two or three thousand people, most of them on foot or bicycle, would turn out if the weather was fine.

Among them were the Druids who turned up annually to perform their rituals. When Stonehenge was fenced off and admission charged by the private landowner in the early 1900s the Druids protested. Only after many years

A free festival grew up around Stonehenge during the last century

were they finally able to carry out their ceremonies inside the circle again.

By the 1950s the Druids were an accepted part of the solstice experience, but were often squashed and jostled by the ever-increasing crowds who were enjoying the party atmosphere with music and alcohol.

During the 1970s the crowds began to stay for longer than just the solstice night. Fields nearby were taken over by thousands of campers up to a week before the event, and many stayed on after as well.

Although there were no organisers, posters advertising the free festival began to appear and

Summer sunrise

the event drew larger and larger crowds. It became a magnet for hippies and travellers and for them it was the social highlight of the year.

There were many problems caused by the gathering of so many people on an unorganised site. Litter, the lack of adequate toilet facilities and erosion caused by the increased footfall were high on the list and by the mid-eighties the authorities and local farmers had had enough.

In 1985 it was decided to stop the festival and police put up a roadblock on the road to Stonehenge. The convoy of travellers was watched closely and as it got bigger extra police were drafted in from neighbouring counties.

The festivalgoers were outraged at being told they could not have access and the result was

People have watched the midsummer sunrise at Stonehenge for centuries

an extremely violent confrontation that became known as the 'Battle of the Beanfield'.

After several years of repeated roadblocks it was obvious the authorities were not going to back down and groups drifted off to other festivals such as Glastonbury or to celebrate more quietly at other stone circles like Avebury.

Fifteen years later English Heritage quietly reopened Stonehenge for the solstice on condition that everyone left before the site opened for business in the morning. Since then the numbers celebrating have gradually been increasing every year.

Sunset